A.EYE
CANDY

A MUSEUM OF IMAGINARY ROBOTS AND OTHER DIGITAL DELIGHTS

LANGUAGE IN
ACTION SERIES

COREY ANTON

The **INSTITUTE**
of **GENERAL**
SEMANTICS

Published by the Institute of General Semantics
www.generalsemantics.org

Cover & Interior Book Design by Scribe Freelance
www.scribefreelance.com

Published in the United States of America

ISBN: 978-1-970164-26-8

Library of Congress Cataloging-in-Publication Data

Names: Anton, Corey, artist, writer of added text.
Title: A.EYE candy : a museum of imaginary robots and other digital
 delights / Corey Anton.
Other titles: A I candy : a museum of imaginary robots and other digital
 delights
Description: Forest Hills, New York : The Institute of General Semantics,
 [2023] | Series: Language in action series | Includes bibliographical
 references. | Summary: "Sure to dazzle your senses and inspire your
 imagination, A.EYE CANDY presents some deliciously bizarre, intriguing
 and weird images. It includes a variety of different robots, robots that
 are creating art, strange and odd imaginary creatures, and abstract
 "art-like" images. This lovely collection will keep you coming back
 again and again with an increased delight in every viewing. For anyone
 interested in imaginary robots, robot artists, surreal animals, abstract
 art, and/or the generative AI revolution, this "must have" coffee table
 book offers an absolute treasure trove"-- Provided by publisher.
Identifiers: LCCN 2023028897 | ISBN 9781970164268 (paperback)
Subjects: LCSH: Anton, Corey--Themes, motives. | AI art--Themes, motives. |
 Fantasy in art.
Classification: LCC N7433.85.A58 A4 2023 | DDC 776--dc23/eng/20230824
LC record available at https://lccn.loc.gov/2023028897

Poetry often conveys in a few sentences more of lasting value than a whole volume of scientific analysis.
—ALFRED KORZYBSKI

The **Language in Action** series, sponsored by the Institute of General Semantics, publishes books devoted to creative modes of expression that can open the doors of perception, and foster better understandings of the nature of language, symbols, communication, and the semantic, technological, and media environments that we inhabit. Through processes of play and probing, art can bring into awareness alternative forms of experience and evaluation to the everyday, routine, taken-for-granted world. It can also shed new light on mind and method, consciousness and culture, abstracting and attention, ecology and enlightenment, and, most important to students of general semantics, science and sanity.

Founded in 1938 by Alfred Korzybski, the Institute of General Semantics promotes, in the words of S.I. Hayakawa, *the study of how not to be a damn fool*. As a non-aristotelian system devoted to enhancing human potential, general semantics has inspired numerous novelists, poets, artists, musicians, and creative thinkers. General semantics today is devoted to explorations of meaning and the meaning of meaning, of metaphors and memes, archetypes and arts, symbols and signals, signs and significance, codes and ciphers, sense perception and sense-making, and the vast variety of ways of seeing, feeling, and thinking that humanity is heir to. The quarterly journal of the IGS, *ETC: A Review of General Semantics*, has been publishing essays, research, and literary work since 1943.

Other titles included in the Language in Action Series
Lance Strate, Series Editor

Strate, Lance (2020). *Diatribal Writes of Passage in a World of Wintertextuality: Poems on Language, Media, and Life (But Not as We Know It)*

Levinson, Martin H., with Photography by Katherine Liepe-Levinson (2020). *Signal Reactions and Other Poems*

Karasick, Adeena (2022). *Massaging the Medium: Seven Pechakuchas*

Praise for A.EYE CANDY

"In this lively book, Corey Anton reminds us that AI can be productively employed to stimulate the imagination. The sophisticated, often goofy (often both) characters are funny, tragic, creative and unique. The 'Imaginary art exhibition' contains kaleidoscopic images which resist definition in the same way that great artworks resist definition. Whether you approach this book as a collection of artworks, or a compendium of AI imagery - *A.EYE Candy* is an entertaining exploration of the modern hybrid imagination."

—Dom Heffer, Artist (UK)

"In his uniquely brilliant way, Corey Anton has crafted *A.EYE Candy* to advance both wisdom about the explosion of generative AI and inspiration for its use. By thoughtfully and expertly exploring the potential of AI as its own artistic medium, Anton has brought forth emotionally evocative and appealing imagery, inviting us all to suspend judgment of AI's capabilities and partake in intriguing new ways of creating, seeing and knowing."

—Julianne Newton, Professor of Visual Communication & Director of the Communication and Media Studies Doctoral Program, University of Oregon

"Prepare to go fishing with Corey Anton. In his introduction, Anton advances fishing as a helpful metaphor for the process of tweaking and refining the prompts that reeled in all the gorgeous AI-generated images in this book. And what a museum they comprise: a potent cocktail of whimsy and nightmare fuel. You'll see robots, robot artists, a bestiary beyond human imagining, and abstract spaces where forms struggle to assert themselves. Is it art? With a general semanticist's distrust of the copula of identity, Anton unasks that question, choosing to foreground human intent, which was "to generate images that are aesthetically pleasing." Whether you're gazing in wonder at Escher-y scenes, considering an armadillo-tardigrade chimera or puzzling out the Bosch-like forms slithering through less figurative pieces, you're sure to find something that challenges your perceptions in interesting ways. So grab the chum bucket and get ready to experience the rapture of the deep."

—John McDaid, Adjunct Professor, Roger Williams University

TABLE OF CONTENTS

ACKNOWLEDGMENTS

Many people at GVSU need to be acknowledged and thanked. I am grateful for the kind permission to use Grand Valley's resources in the production of this book, in particular, the computer lab in Lake Superior Hall. Especially instrumental behind the scenes were Pam De Windt, Robin Getz, and Jim Schaub. I am greatly indebted to them for their support and assistance. I also want to recognize the current provost at GVSU, Fatma Mili, who during the winter semester of 2023 put together a panel discussion regarding CHAT-GPT and invited me to participate. This project was partly encouraged by those early discussions. I should also state that I have many wonderful colleagues at Grand Valley, and a few who saw the collection prior to publication and to whom I am grateful include: Richard Besel, Len O'Kelly, Anthony Spencer, and Robert Swieringa.

I want to thank Daniel J. Middleton at Scribe Freelance for assistance, guidance and suggestions. I also should acknowledge Tiffany Petricini for some early discussions regarding CHAT-GPT. She helped me engage with these kinds of technologies.

I need to thank the Institute of General Semantics (IGS) for their continued support, encouragement, and inspiration. And I should add here that all royalties from this book are being donated to the IGS. I also need to recognize the Media Ecology Association (MEA). The IGS and the MEA have given me so much over the years. I am grateful to have such tight affiliations with the people in these intellectually robust and stimulating organizations. I especially want to single out and acknowledge my colleagues Lance

Strate, Thom Gencarelli, Eva Berger, Nora Bateson, Susan J. Drucker, and Mike Plugh.

A good number of friends have helped me in evaluating, culling, arranging, and generally thinking about the collection. Some people who have seen the images pre-publication and who I would like to recognize are: the many good folks at both Burzurk Brewery in Grand Haven, especially Tyler Forbes and Karen Alondra Forbes, and The Unicorn Tavern in Grand Haven, especially Garry and Kristal Boyd, and CJ Boyd. I also want to thank Grace E. Peterson, Valorie Putnam, Matt Wass, Kim Helmers, Evan Breen, Brian Esparsa, Damon Esparsa, Lynn Brouwer, Jeremy and Polly Czarniak, Jamie Cross, Tom McCarthy, Stacy Shultz Dodson, Steve Barnes, Brent and Marge Newville, Toby and Becky Moleski, Joanie Latsch, Randi Gonzalez, Alex Achterhof, Dirk and Gail Heinemann, Mark Zuidema, Lee Woodruff and Wenqi Woodruff, Lindsay Robbins, Don Carter, Jean and Tim Cuddington, Rich and Char Vander Stel, Ken Sapkowski, Glenda Eikenberry, Jan and Marty Blanchard, Josh Larabee, Thomas Saukas, Kyle Krause, Dave Snyder, Brian Burns, Tracy Ziska, Brecken McClain, Cassidy Harper, Stephen Matchett, Justin Frederick, Tom Eagle, Chris and John Helder, Tom Cleveland, Daniel Powers, Nick VanderMeiden, and Tacitus Abeshi.

Additional friends should be mentioned and thanked for discussions relating to some of these images, including: Bryan Wehr, Phil Paradowski, Barry Liss, Chad Hansen and Jermaine Martinez.

The students in my winter semester 2023 COM 641: Emerging Communication Technologies course were with me at the beginning of the rise of GPT technologies, and were both directly and indirectly instrumental in motivating my project. I here want to recognize them by name: Esi Aniwa, Cesar Ayala-Orellana, Joshua Borger, Brendann Brown, Isaiah Carver-Bagley, Andrew Christian, William Cuppy, Isabell David, Rachel Davis, Steven Fitzek, Margaret Hammer, Daniel Kiely, Jay McBride, Chinedu Okanu, Daniel Rikkers, Brian Roberts, Riley Sweet, Joseph Tekelly, and Savannah Thompson.

I also wish to thank Valerie V. Peterson for endless care and encouragement. As I think many people can imagine, this book project has been an exhausting process. I need to acknowledge that Valerie has been there for me with intellectual insight, emotional support, and helpful suggestions. I could not have done it without her.

WELCOME TO THE MUSEUM

Welcome to *A.EYE CANDY: A Museum of Imaginary Robots and Other Digital Delights*. You here will discover many appealing and captivating images. Although the images can be enjoyed anywhere, they best show themselves in direct sunlight. I hope that you find them interesting and intriguing. Some of them you might even think of as "art."

All of the images presented here, except one, were generated on an artificial intelligence system called "Stable Diffusion 2.1," partly through the help of another AI system called, "Clip Interrogator." Both systems were accessed through the AI developer site called "Hugging Face." A wide variety of AI systems can be found on Hugging Face (over 2,000 of them), but, broadly construed, two main types handle image generation. One type turns verbal prompts into images (e.g.

Stable Diffusion 2.1), and the other type takes images and generates prompts designed to produce something similar to the original image (e.g. Clip Interrogator). The latter is more challenging and time-consuming for computers, because images contain many times more data-points than a few phrases could ever convey. As of April 2023, Clip Interrogator seems less useful than intuition in creating prompts that generate desired images, but, it is quite helpful in establishing a general sense of the range of possible prompts. Playing back and forth between both kinds of systems is an enlightening exercise: it helps people learn how to prompt the AI and how to generate better images. It also encourages reflection on the many differences between words and images.

Both kinds of AI systems are "generative"

AI. They require what is called "prompt engineering." Prompt engineering means using precise words, phrases, expressions, styles, genres, artists, etc. to generate what you want to see and don't want to see. There are positive prompts, which tell the AI what to generate, and negative prompts, which specify what not to generate. In my prompt engineering, I avoided some of the more popular strategies; I was rather strict. For example, I did not use the name of any artist (e.g. Michelangelo or Salvador Dali), nor did I use the name of any media conglomerate or corporate entity (e.g. Pixar or Disney), nor did I use any TV show or movie (*Futurama* or *Star Wars*). My positive prompts were descriptive along the lines of: "a unique robot that is creating art while standing upon a wooden table, very realistic, photorealistic character-design," etc. Negative prompts were equally descriptive and categorical: "sketch, comic, cartoon, blurry" etc. That said, both positive and negative prompts were at times lengthy, complex, and highly elaborated.

The process of making the images was somewhat like "magical" digital fishing. This fishing requires the right "lure," the right kind of "net" and the right "places" to go. It requires patience, occasionally changing lures, moving to different waters and sometimes trying different depths. But the fishing metaphor only goes so far, for there are no specific fish in the area until the net is dropped. There were, of course, all of those original images that were used to train the AI systems; it is a veritable ocean. Nevertheless, the point here is that the prompts are not grabbing already existing images and sharing them; they're not simply modifying images one at a time. Generative AI systems do massive and very strange work: they use words to disperse and then solidify and concretize images: they render by generating actualities out of what were merely possibilities prior to the prompt. This is some enchanted fishing to be sure.

The image-generating process is also a little similar to looking for shells along the seashore. Once again, a kind of "magic" seems to be at play: the shells only appear as you approach and look for them. They get generated and washed up according to the waves the prompts make. Like shelling, it's easy to start eager. Low standards soon lead to a massive collection. But as the shells become more familiar, the collector gets more discerning and discriminating. Then, only the best or rarest shells are added to the collection.

For some of the reasons just mentioned

(and others still to be mentioned), I consider myself to be the author of this book, but I tend not to see myself as an "Artist" behind these images. In my mind, the "real artists" are the individuals—painters, photographers, sculptors, etc.—whose work became the sea of verbal data-points that trained the AI systems. Others behind the scene likely do not see themselves as artists either, despite the fact that they were instrumental in making these images possible. They are the computer developers, programmers and digital architects who played a hand in creating Stable Diffusion. These technologies, as well as the images they generate, offer exemplars of what Alfred Korzybski (2001) meant by "wealth" in his theory of "time-binding." We find here a wealth that is many generations in the making, most of it the fruit of the toil of people long since dead. Stable Diffusion accomplished a deep intermingling of art, language, history and science to produce a superabundance of aesthetic wealth now available at the push of a few buttons.

Admittedly, these particular images would not exist if I did not prompt them into existence; I did need to push some buttons to generate them. And, I should add that it took considerable time to generate, select, compile, and arrange them. There are also some "artistic" embellishments here and there, including one hidden treasure of original art. I also should acknowledge that I greatly benefitted from the expertise of a digital media specialist colleague, Jim Schaub, who assisted in the final stages. He not only converted the images from their original resolution of 72 DPI to the needed, and much richer, resolution of 300 DPI, but, he used "Neural filters" within Adobe Photoshop 2023, powered by Adobe Sensei to clean and tighten near all of the images. I think of this as similar to washing and polishing shells after you've left the beach and now have them back home. Sure, they looked great out along the shoreline, but now they look even better after they've been cleaned up and polished. Without the ability to covert them to 300 DPI, this book could not have come into existence, and, for this reason, it seems even more of a collective product to which I have become the custodian.

I use the metaphor of "museum" for this book because I feel more like the curator of exotic items and of collective riches, more like the caretaker of relics obtained from unknown others and far away places. The book also feels like a museum because these AI systems are changing and evolving at an ever-quickening rate. By the time this collection is printed there will be newer and superior AI systems. Things move so fast in the AI world that anyone making images quickly becomes an antique dealer. I experienced some of this while working on this project. The seas themselves change; the systems get updated. Now, in retrospect, the images here seem as quaint and old-fashioned as they seem weird and surreal.

I know that some people despise AI images and ridicule the expression, "AI art." Many professional artists, people who work with oil paints, clay, glass, etc., and people who "do art" for a living, think that the expression "AI art" trivializes and belittles the creative work "real artists" do. They furthermore think that the expression aggrandizes what amounts to "button pushing." Some believe that people who generate AI images traffic in shallow activities bereft of artistic substance. Digital images, such people contend, are a degenerate form of expression— one that lacks self-discipline, cultivation of talent, and overall artistic abilities. In some ways, I both agree and yet also disagree with those sentiments.

Let me start with my agreement: this book was not decades in the making; it didn't take that much time to learn how to do the prompt engineering. And, I don't think the images here are of serious cultural or social importance. They are not trying to advance a political cause or serve a grander purpose. They are indulgences, eye candy, something meant for fun and aesthetic pleasure. If the images have any redeeming value, it comes as a solid demonstration of the wealth available at the fingertips of those who have a computer and Internet access. They emerged for me personally with the swell of generative AI systems in 2023. I routinely teach a graduate course titled, "Emerging Communication Technologies," and, in the winter semester of 2023, AI just seemed to be a dominant topic. I discovered "Hugging Face," and the images collected here are the outcome of my attempt to understand what a couple of these AI systems can do. And, I should add that, at least in the past, I have never really thought of photography as a serious or "real" art form. Photography, especially nature photography, seemed more like a technique of capturing beauty already there. To me, it always seemed less creative and less artistic than painting or sculpting. That is perhaps part of the rationale of people who dislike photographs, especially "nature photographs," which are sold as "works of art." Because nature is often immensely beautiful, those who are at the right place and right time can pull out their camera and, despite having little to no creative talent; point, click, and capture the scene. AI generated images are somewhat similar.

On the other hand, and here is my disagreement, these images are difficult to reproduce. They are original, unique, and they did require some amount of patience and skill to create. They demanded more than soulless button pushing. It took some study and homework, some practice and experimentation to come up with the positive and negative prompts (and the advance settings too) that deliver desired results. It is, said otherwise, not absolutely deprived of artistic integrity, certainly not once one considers how any and all artists rely upon learned techniques and tools of the trade: painters, for example, neither make their own brushes nor their own oils nor do they create *ex nihilo*; glass bead makers seldom make their own sticks of glass; those who make tie-dyed shirts very rarely make either their own clothing or their ink, and those who make sculptures out of clay do not themselves produce the clay. Moreover, the many insights, tricks, insider-knowledge accumulated during the processes of doing whatever artists are doing is, all said, the wealth of many generations.

People who are not trained as artists can use generative AI systems to produce images of great beauty, all with little more than some computer keystrokes. And, furthermore, the lack of conscious intent within the AI systems themselves in no way diminishes the beauty of any images they generate. The images can indeed be aesthetically pleasing despite a prompt engineer's lack of artistic training and despite computers' lack of conscious intent. Think of it this way: there are famous, extremely expensive "works of art" created by renown arts, and these works were created with much forethought, creativity, artistic intent, etc., but many people do not find them aesthetically pleasing at all (e.g. Marcel Duchamp's "Fountain"; Jeff Koons' "One Ball Total Equilibrium Tank"). Even though artistic intent may serve as an essential part of some people's definition of "art," it does not necessarily play any vital role in what most people find beautiful.

Marshall McLuhan, over fifty years ago, predicted great changes with the rise of automation (1964). He suggested that automation is most disruptive to "specialists" and "experts" because they, the specialists and the experts, "stay put." In contrast, "amateurs," says McLuhan, can afford to lose. This means that people who are too specialist in their ways may be obsolesced more quickly than they think. As a simple example, I am not a professional artist, but some of the images collected here, especially those in Exhibit Four, seemingly rival works of "great artists." This rather eerie fact evokes the relevant line by McLuhan and Fiore: "'Come into my parlor,' said the computer to the specialist" (1967, p. 20). In this regard, I should also add that it is precisely because I do not see myself as an artist, i.e. because I am an amateur, that I felt rather free to dabble around with these AI systems. In contrast (and in alignment with McLuhan's observations), I am extremely reluctant to allow CHAT-GPT, or any other generative AI writing system, to do my writing for me. As a specialist in writing, I would find that rather disingenuous and phony. I don't want to slum it that way. That said, I fully recognize that some amateur with a generative AI writing system may soon enough be serious competition.

There are four exhibits in this museum of a book. The first one, **A Range of Robots**, covers a few different styles, colors, and kinds of robots. They are meant to whet your appetite and your imagination. They are cute, odd, intriguing, and generally fun to look at. There are bizarre ones, small and large ones, a couple of robotic spiders, and even a few robot couples.

The second exhibit, **Robot Artists**, offers a generous collection of robots making art or standing beside their creations. Robots have long captured the imagination and have been a staple of science fiction. Now, with the endless stream of generative AI products, the emergence of self-driving cars, and various kinds of industrial and service robots, it seemed appropriate to re-imagine robots, this time as artists. Many are making surrealist paintings, some are creating abstract works, and others are making kinds of 3-D sculpture. They serve as the guiding metaphor for this book. They are meant to underscore the fact that AI systems generated all these images, and this fact is rather surreal. "Robots making art" is indeed the metaphorical theme of the book, as all but one of the images here were generated by AI technologies.

The third exhibit, "**Fantastical Animals**," presents a wide array of imaginary animals; it is a contemporary bestiary. Many of the animals are weird to say the least. If you are sharing this book with children, I encourage you to ask them what kinds of sounds each pictured organism would likely make.

All of them, perhaps obviously, are on the imaginary endangered species list (as they are extremely rare), but, if any hunters are out there, two animals can be found on neighboring pages, ("cow deer duck" and "flying deer"), which are sometimes targeted for hunting, assuming that hunters have the required licenses and permits. I should stress that the legal hunting season for "cow deer duck" and for "flying deer" is during the third week of February through the first week of March during a leap year, after 4 am but before 7 am. Other restrictions may apply depending upon your area.

Besides all of the mystification and commercial hype surrounding AI systems in 2023, one of the most significant scientific discoveries made by AI systems concerns how proteins fold. AI has accomplished in a few months what otherwise would have taken many years. This is, without a doubt, a revolutionary discovery, and it has profound and far-reaching implications for genetic research and for humans' relationship with nature and themselves. People should not anticipate the existence of any of the fantastical animals presented here, but these animals serve as a visual reminder of how much of nature and the processes of evolution are now orchestrated by human interventions. Highly sophisticated and creative forms of genetic engineering, increasingly powered by AI systems, are just around the corner.

Exhibit Four, "**Imaginary Art Installation**," offers a series of highly abstract AI generated images. This exhibit requires your imagination. You need to imagine that you are in a museum and it is showcasing an exhibit on abstract art. In that space, these images line the walls. Imagine that they are large high-quality paintings: six foot high and five foot wide. You also should imagine that you have all the time in the world (and the patience) to scrutinize each image at length.

Regarding these "imaginary art" images, I should point out a fact relating again to the issue of "artistic intent." ALL of these "imaginary art installation" images were created with the *exact* same prompts that were used to generate either the images of robots making art or of fantastical animals. (At first, these were what I was seeking). Again: the same exact prompts were used. The only difference was a change I made in the "Advanced Settings," called the "Guidance

Scale," which varies from "0" to "50," with "9" set as the default. When I used the default, which is a "tight leash" of instruction, the system consistently generated the intended images. If I lowered the number a little bit, say to "7.8" or to "5.3," the system generated my intended images a little less consistently but with more realism. But, then, when I radically lowered the guidance scale, bringing it under "1" (e.g. between ".2" and ".5"), it mostly generated messy wreckage, a certain subset of which are on display in Appendix A. On rare occasions (to my great surprise and out of obvious alignment with the prompt), abstract images such as those found in Exhibit Four would show up. This means that these images were not what I initially was "attempting" to generate via the prompt. It was like going out fishing for lobsters, dropping down lobster traps, and hauling up lots of lobsters, but then also discovering that these same lobster traps, when dropped in different waters, occasionally haul up not lobsters but sunken treasure. I like to think of these as coming up from the unconscious reservoir, the murky depths of data resources. This is like fishing in the middle of the ocean in the deepest of waters. Great patience is required. I am confident some people will find these images beautiful. Should they be called "art"? Well, they drew from a massive stock of art, images, photographs, etc., and *I was intending* to generate images that are aesthetically pleasing. Ultimately, I leave it for readers to decide for themselves if any of these images qualify as art to them.

The entire experience of generating images and producing the book was an adventure. There were many days, too many, where I spent the bulk of the day examining countless different images. Many had juxtaposed 2-dimensional and 3-dimensional elements, and many contained surrealistic imagery. It was like doing a battery of eye calisthenics. My eyes got quite a workout, so much so that my field of vision has changed. My visual field seems brighter and more intense. Contrasts are sharper, almost like objects stand in bas relief. It's been an amazing experience. I can only imagine what will happen to perception and consciousness as more and more people regularly use these kinds of technologies.

Many of the images presented here have a good deal "happening" within them so it is easy, upon further inspection, to notice features and elements that passed below awareness upon first inspection. Because there is so much detail within the images, and because the AI systems introduce glitches here and there, and because there are occasionally connections between neighboring pages, the collection allows readers to return again and again, with each viewing offering up previously unnoticed aspects. It can be surprising and it easily leads one to wonder how newly noticed aspects didn't register during the first viewing. In the terminology of Edward Hall (1976), many of the images provide "high-context" information, most especially, the ones in Exhibit Four. They disseminate their message slowly, and they resist any quick sum up.

One of the early abstract images, one I came to classify in a group I called, "Eye Gari," presents so much visual data indefinitely packed and ambiguously arranged that it defies any clear and articulate statement as to what, exactly, is being shown. Each Eye Gari image has a feel and vibe, and they routinely suggest outlines of bodies or movements and gestures. But these images utterly overflow any definitive statement as to what is "there" and they do not seem to be what most people would call "art." See Appendix A. These kinds of images—and they occur rather regularly out in the deepest of waters—somewhat precipitate a heightening

of consciousness if only momentarily. They illustrate, as Paul Watzlawick (1977) might say, the "benefits of confusion." These images offer eye and judgment exercises—means for seeing the world afresh without the encumbrance of familiar categories and already known objects. Such images force people to look and look again. Much of general semantics demands that people turn their attention to non-verbal levels, including the silent level of observation. Appendix A provides a reminder of the domain of experience that exists prior to categories.

You will notice that there are no names on any of the images. I had attached names to some of them when I began this project, but then, the more I shared the images with different people, the more that names seemed to diminish the viewer's participation in the image; the words seemed to hijack the image.

A final caveat about the future is perhaps in order. The end of 2022 witnessed the release of CHAT- GPT and countless other generative AI systems which captured the popular imagination. 2023 will be remembered as the year that AI systems dominated discussion in the public sphere. Many people rightly express concerns regarding the future. How will all of this AI stuff play out? What does it all mean? Does it promise a techno-utopian age of superabundance? Will it be a world of mega-monopolies and rampant unemployment amidst mass exploitation and social inequality? I am not sure what the answers are here, and I don't think anyone does.

There are always unknown unknowns. I do fear that in making robots appear more human, I am helping to make them seem amusing, cute, and palatable. At times, I did try to counteract the warm and fuzzy feel of some of the images with creepy and menacing tones in other ones. If I am helping to normalize and psychologically soften the massive social disruption caused by robotics, automation, and AI systems, it is perhaps my own conscious and unconscious compulsion to symbolically handle in a simplified way the unprecedented changes that are afoot.

With any luck, the times will change for the better rather than for the worse, and people can kick back and enjoy some digital delights along the way. Susanne K. Langer, citing J. M. Thorburn, writes: "All the genuine, deep delight of life is in showing people the mud-pies you have made; and life is at its best when we confidingly recommend our mud-pies to each other's sympathetic consideration" (1942, p. iii). I hope that readers take some pleasure in these mud-pies.

REFERENCES

Hall, Edward T. (1976). *Beyond Culture*. New York: Anchor Books.

Korzybski, Alfred. (2001). *Manhood of Humanity*. (2nd ed.). Brooklyn, NY: Institute of General Semantics.

Langer, Susanne K. (1942). *Philosophy in a New Key: A Study in the Symbolism of Reason, Rite and Art*. New York: Mentor Books.

McLuhan, Marshall and Quentin Fiore. (1967). *The Medium is the Massage: An Inventory of Effects*. Corte Madera, CA: Ginko Press.

McLuhan, Marshall. (1964). *Understanding Media: Extensions of Man*. Cambridge, MA: The MIT Press.

Watzlawick, Paul. (1977). *How Real is Real?: Confusion, Disinformation, Communication*. New York: Vintage Books.

*To the graduate students
in my COM 641 course
Winter semester, 2023*

Exhibit One

A Range
of
Robots

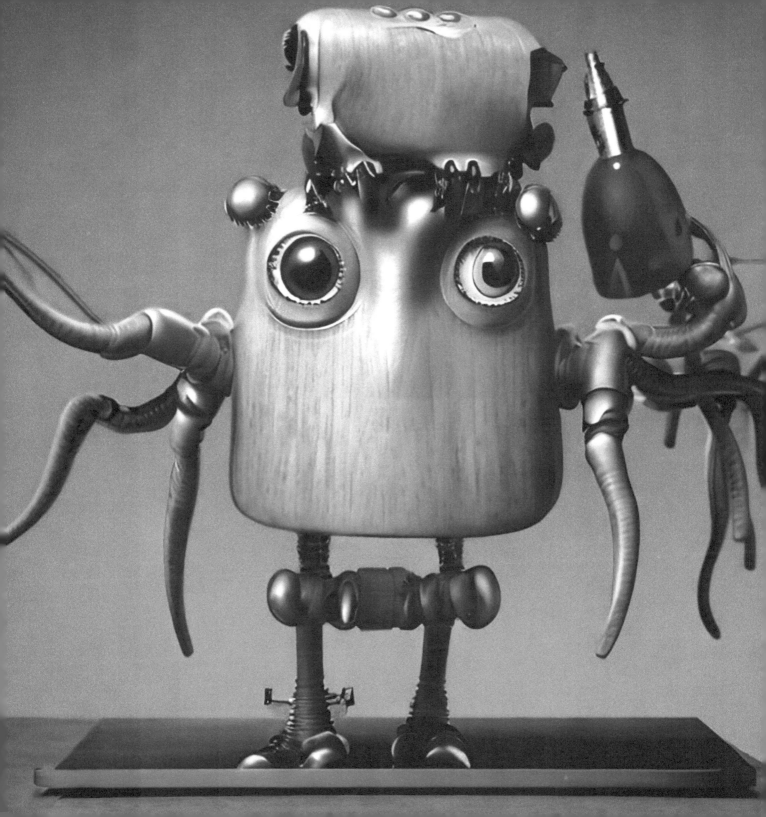

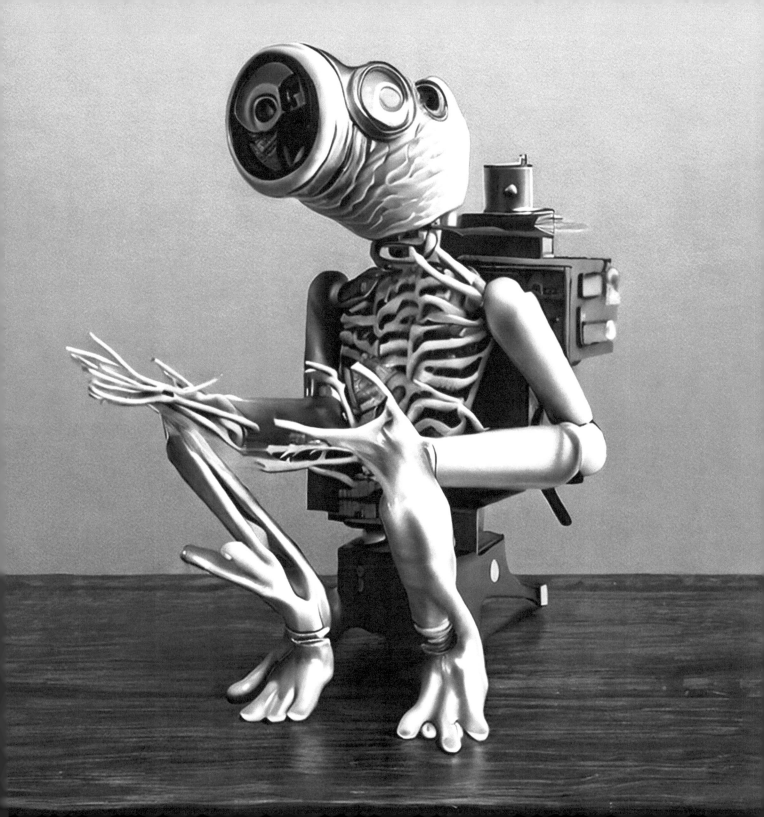

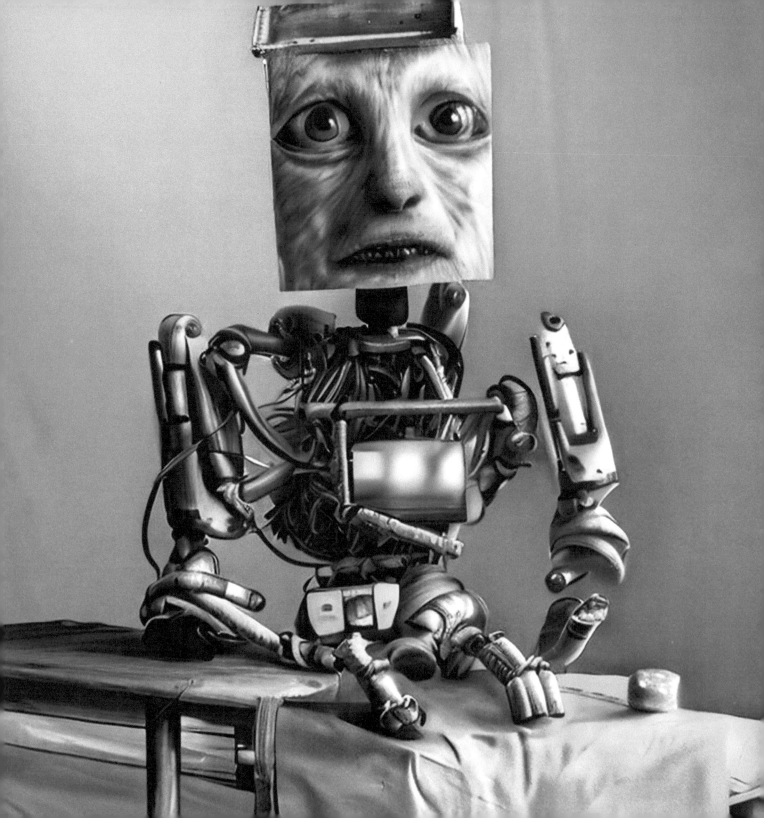

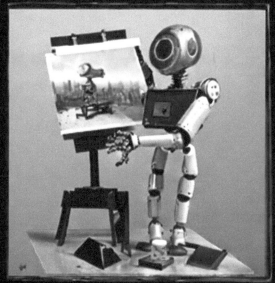

Exhibit Two

Robot Artists

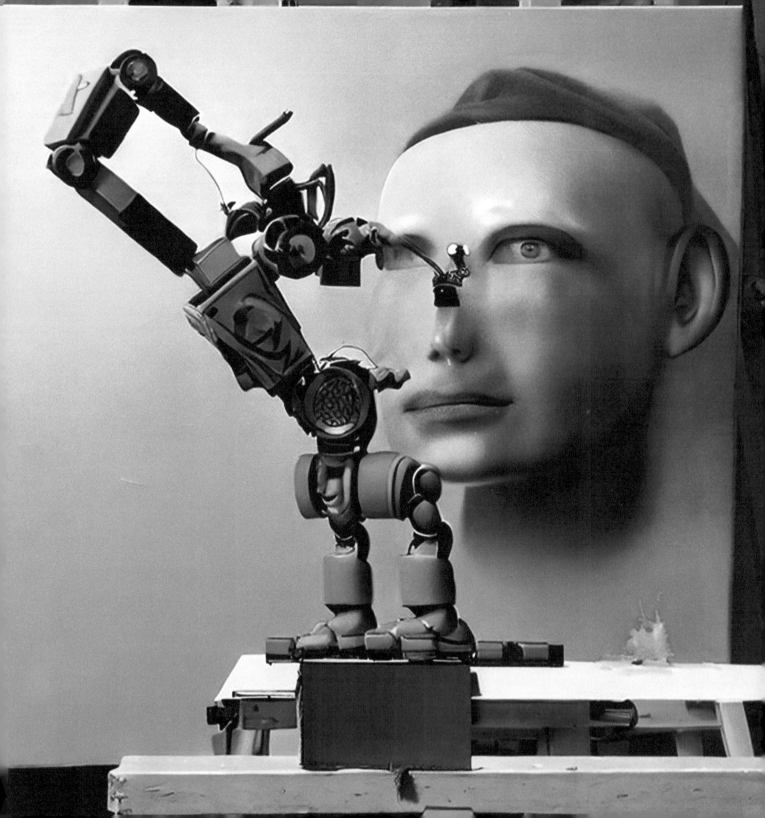

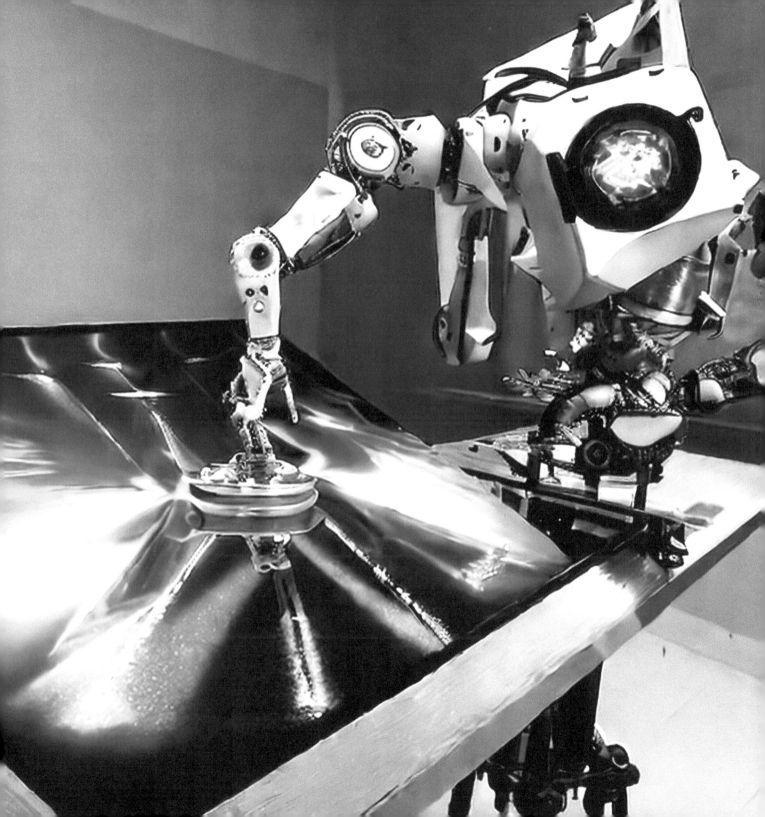

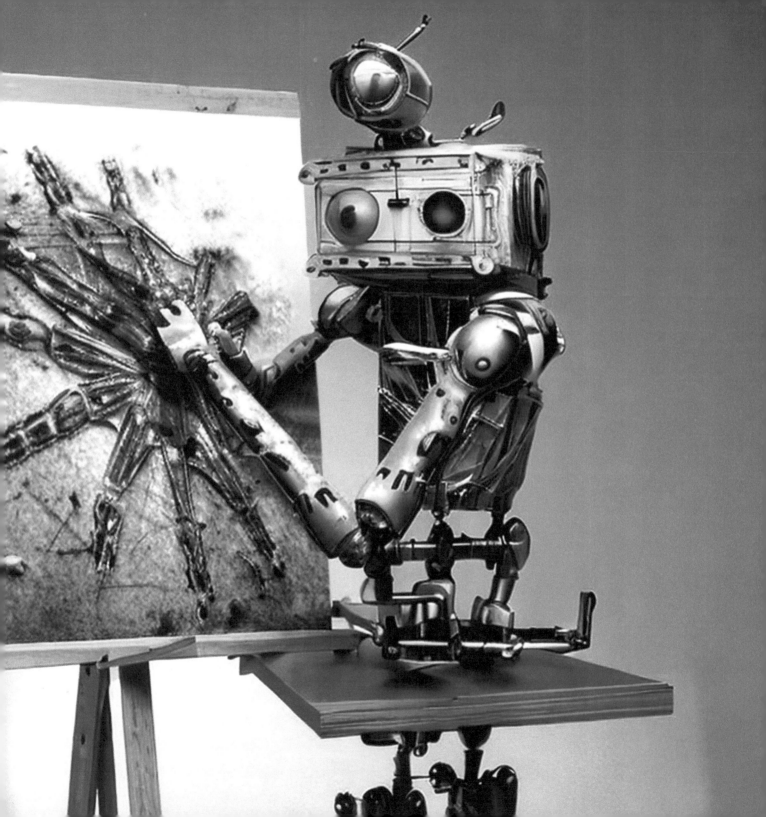

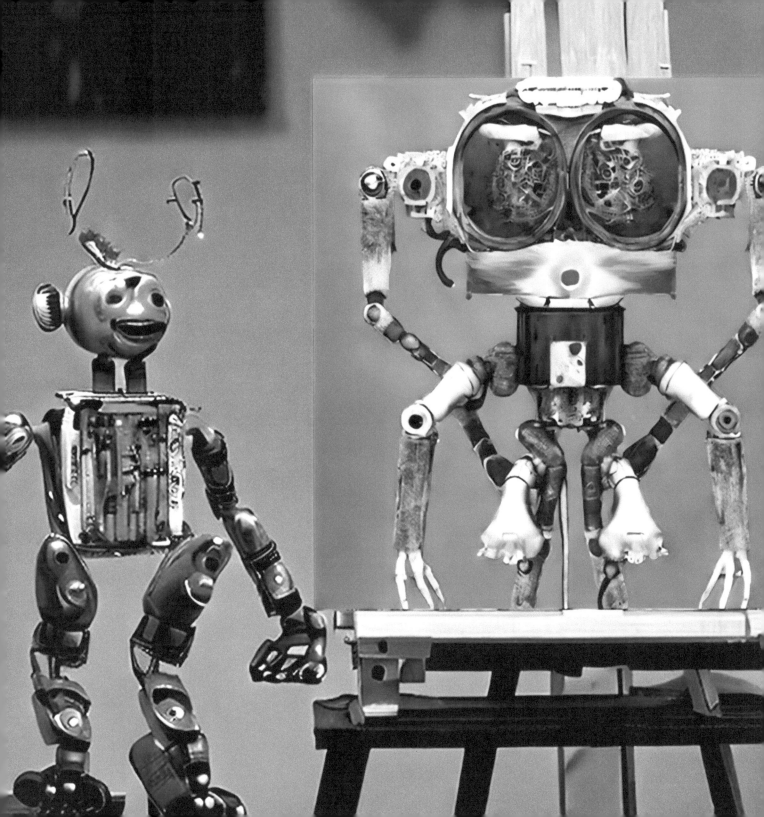

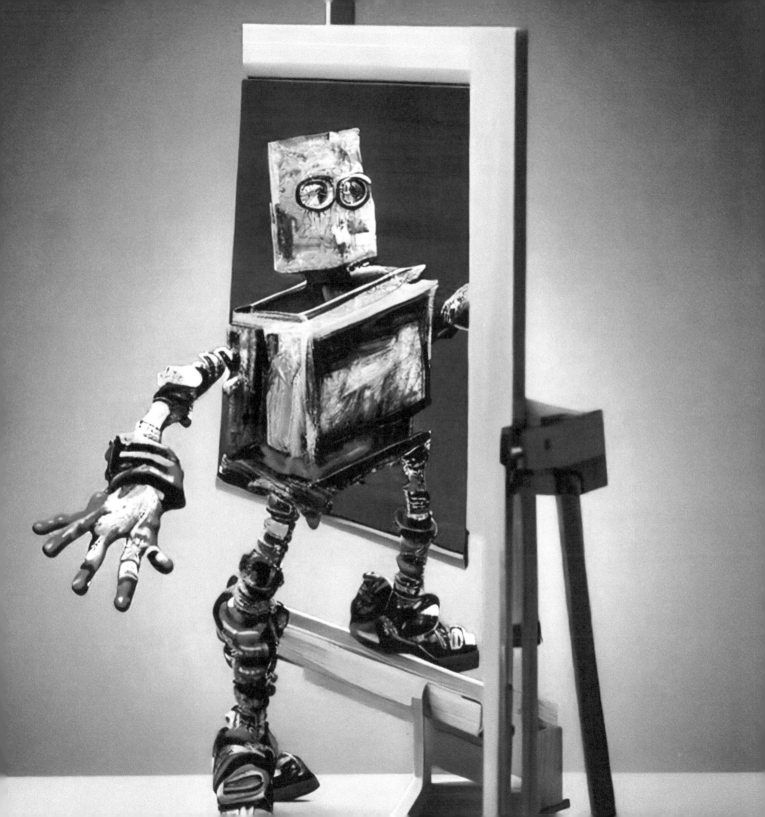

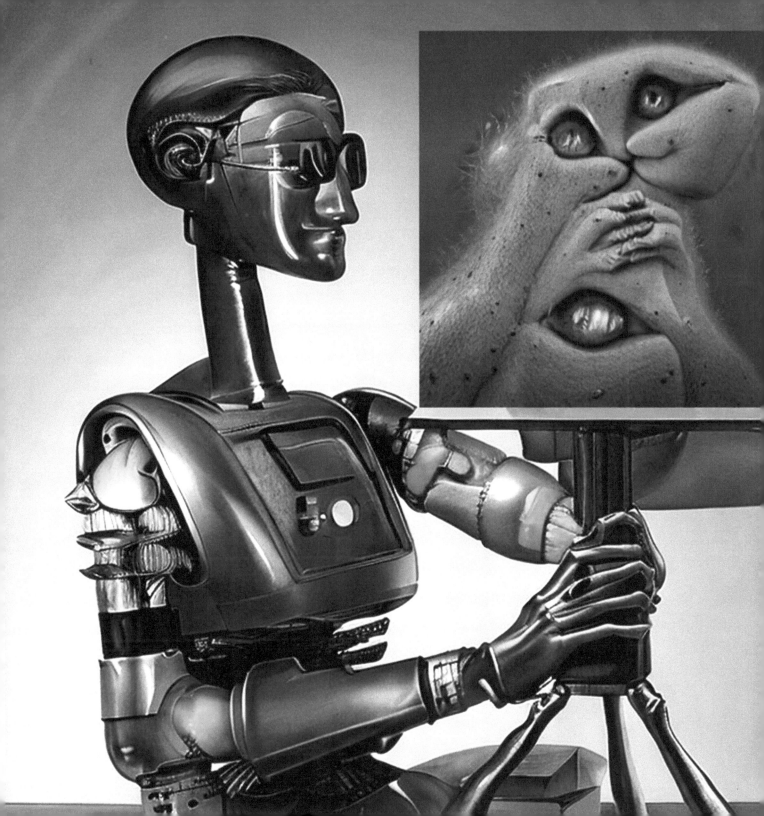

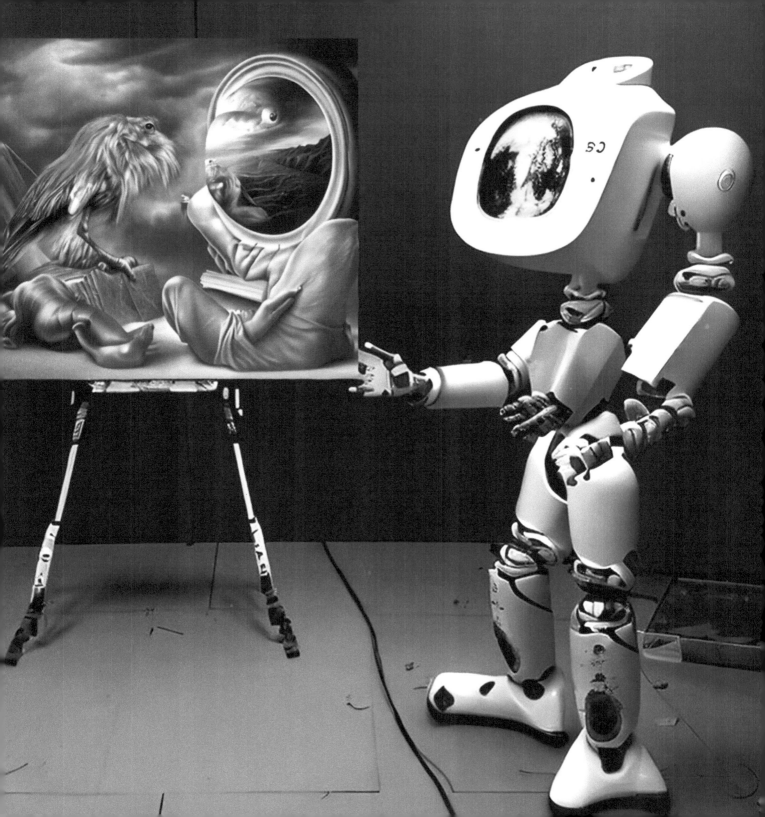

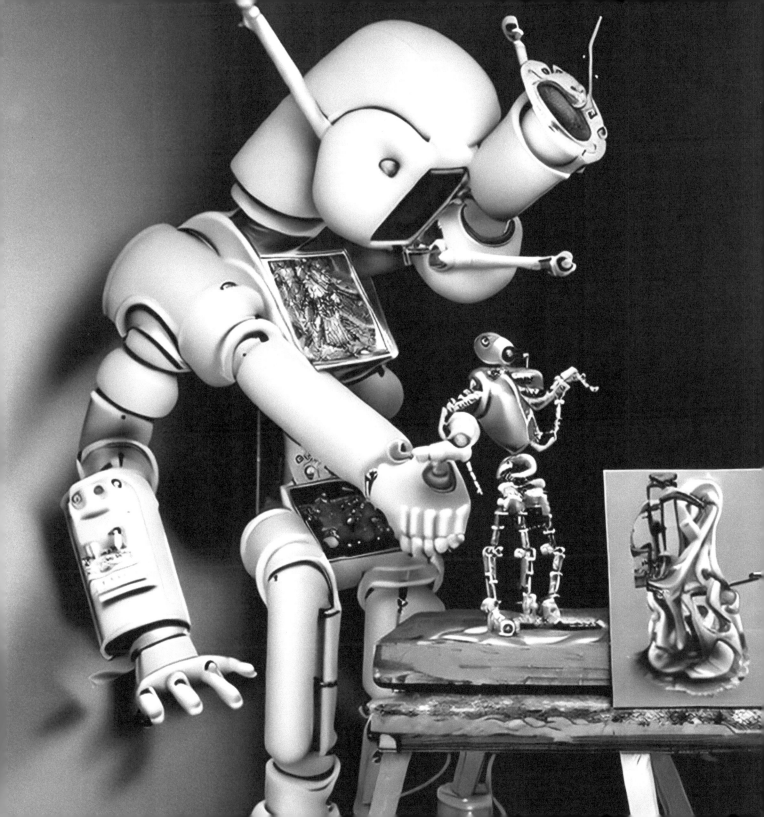

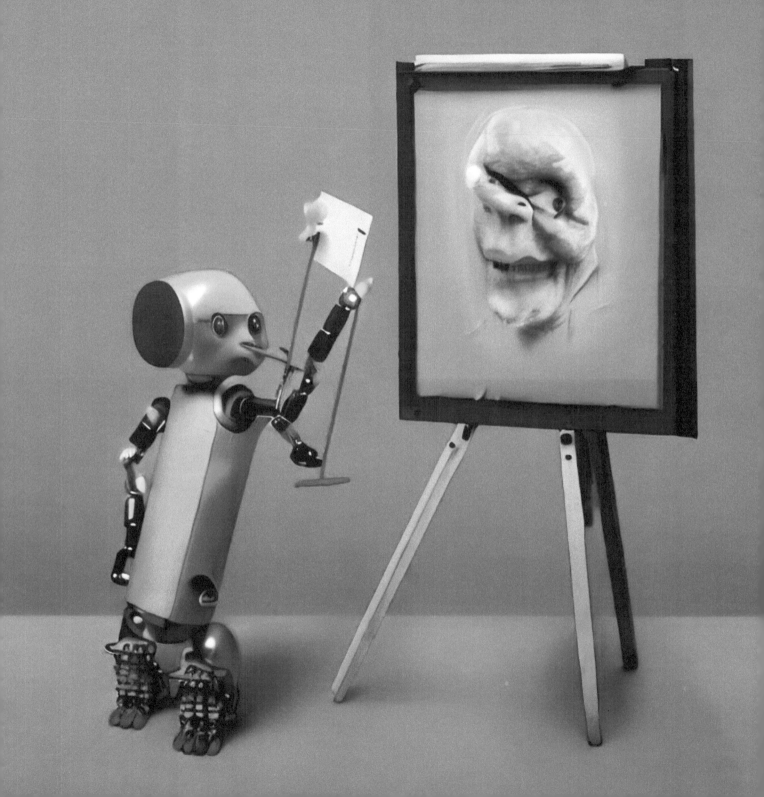

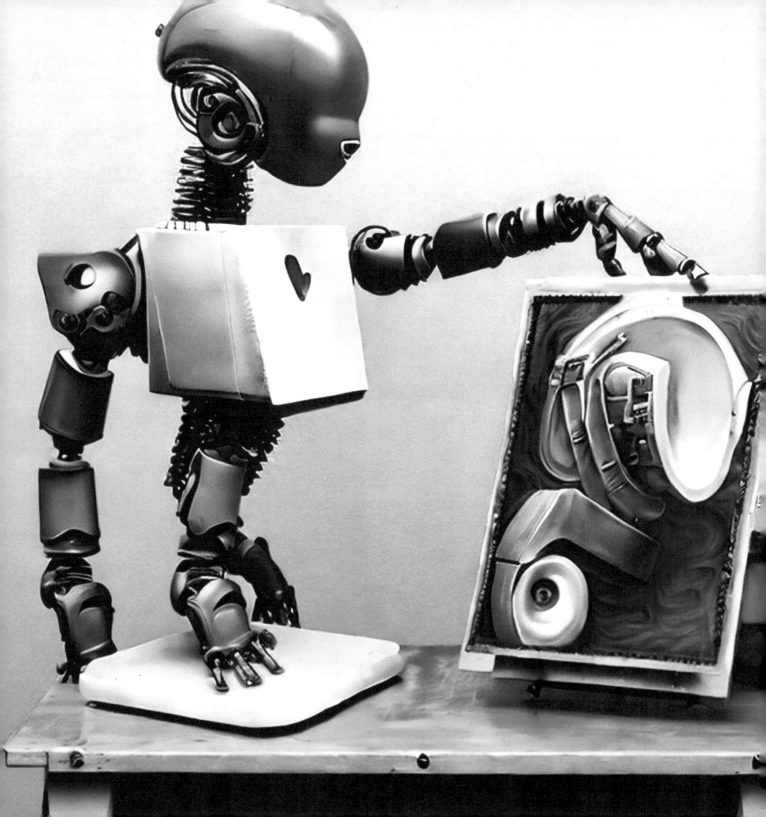

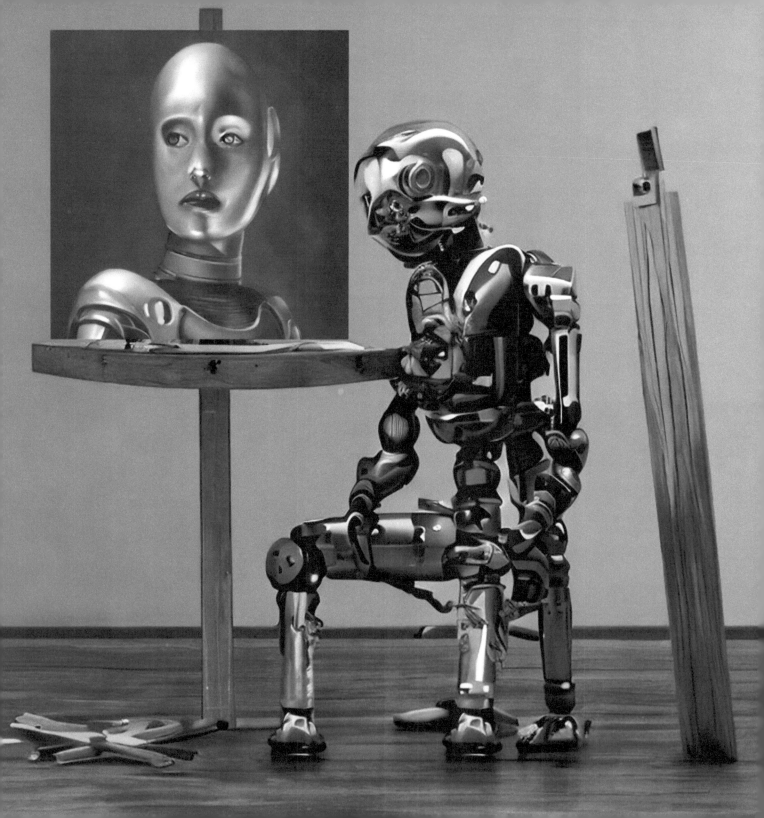

Exhibit Three

Fantastical Animals

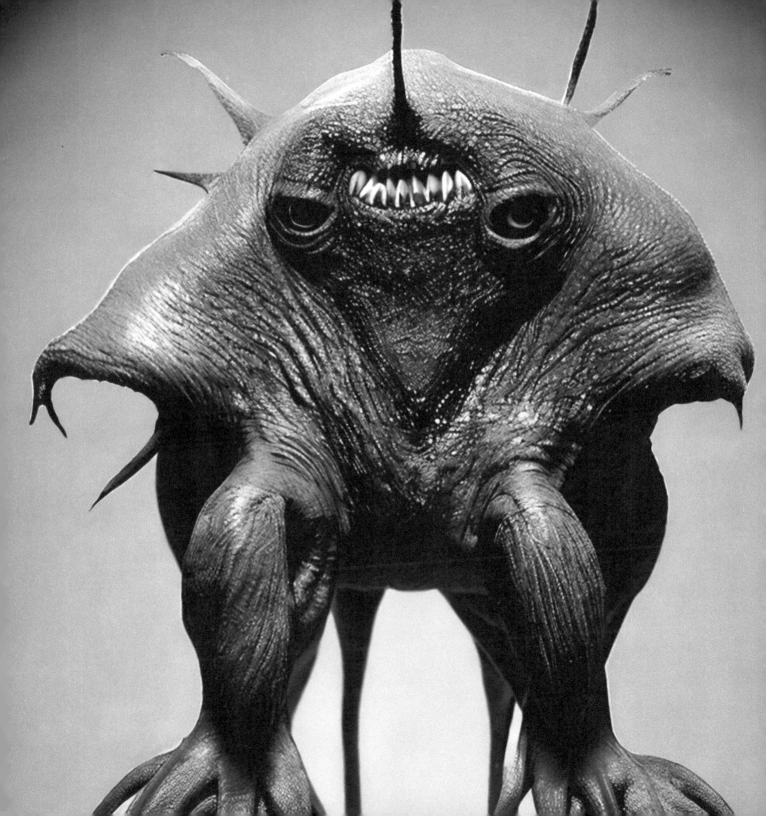

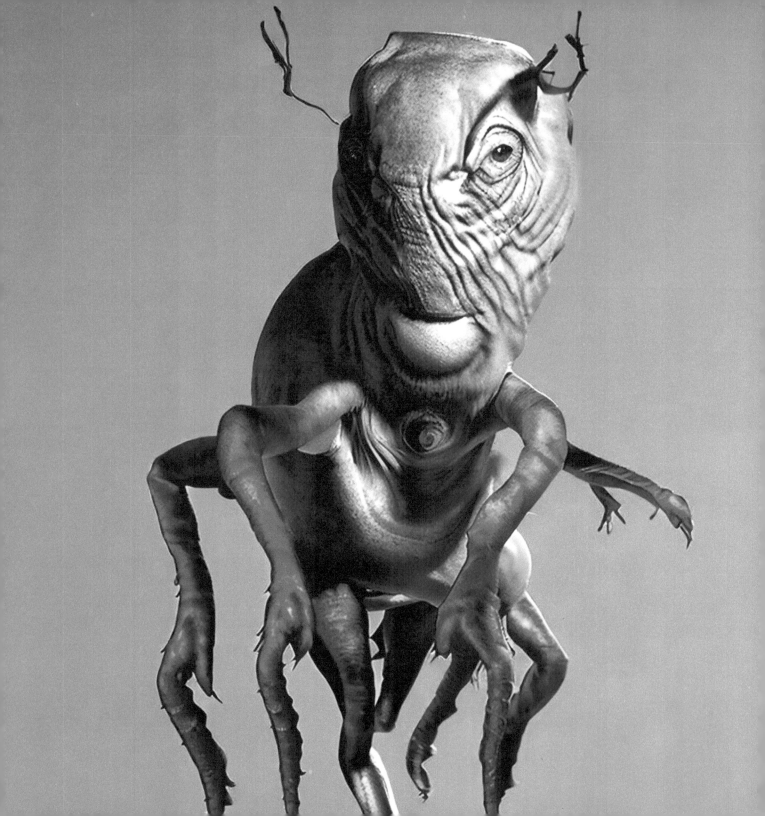

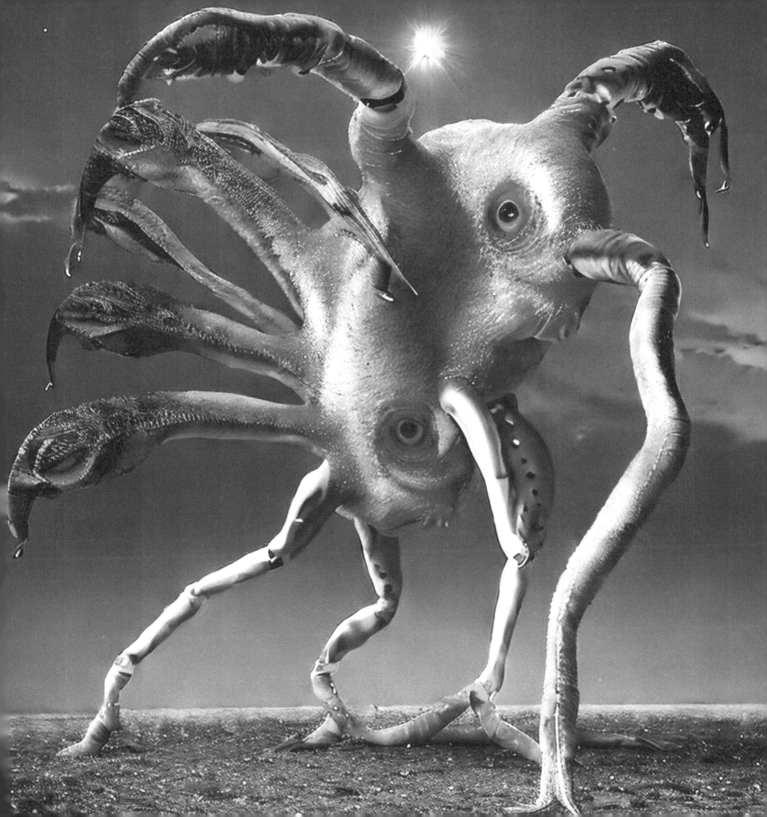

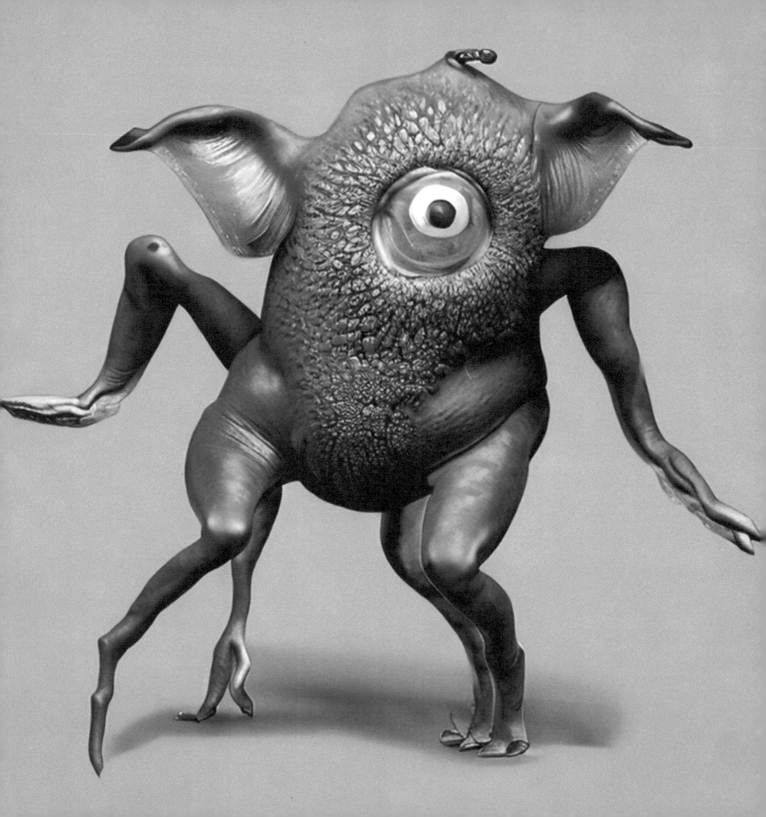

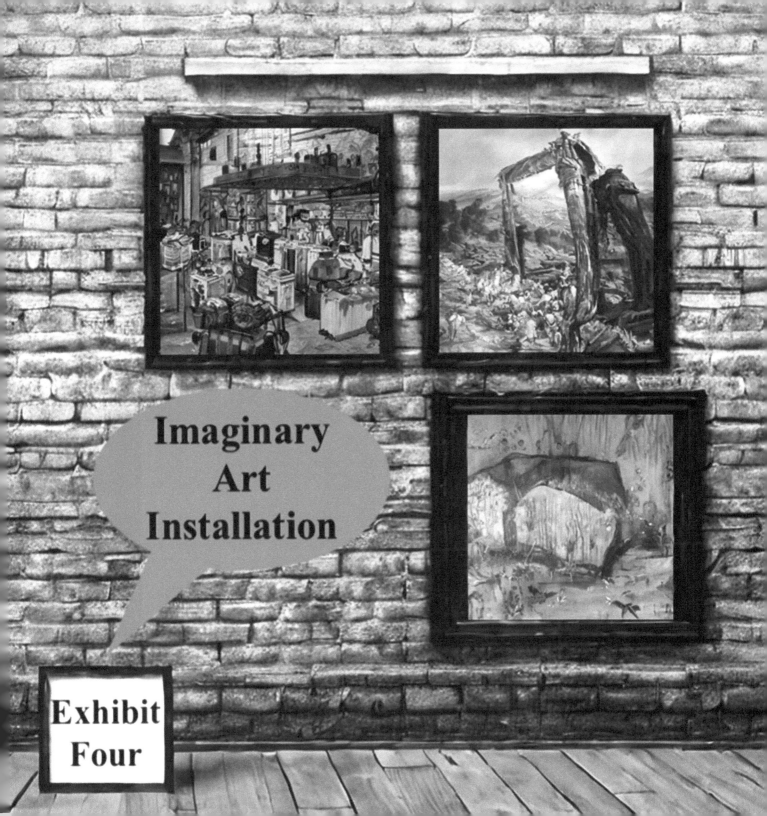

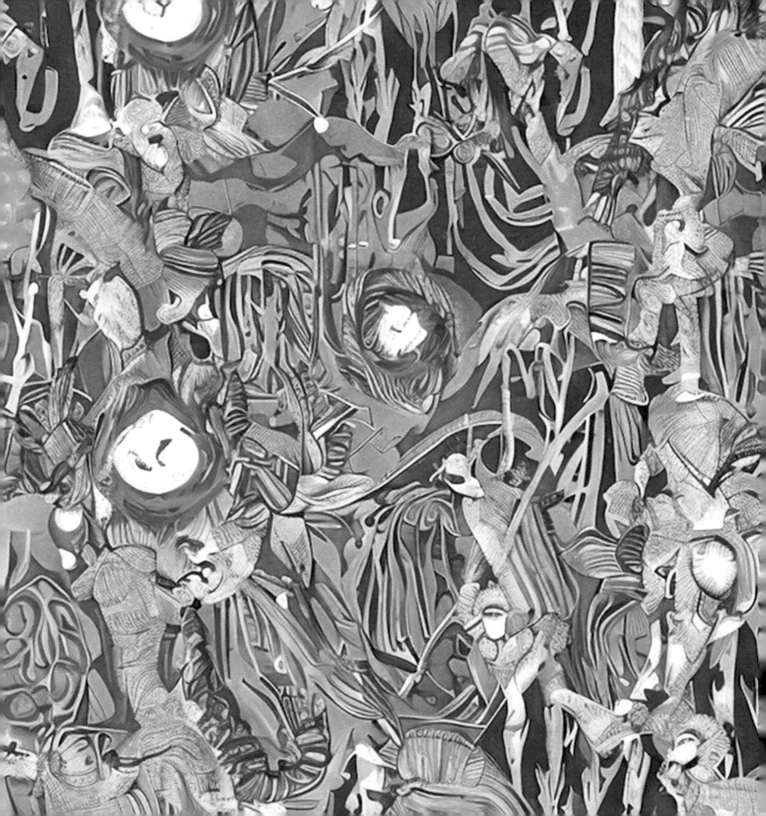

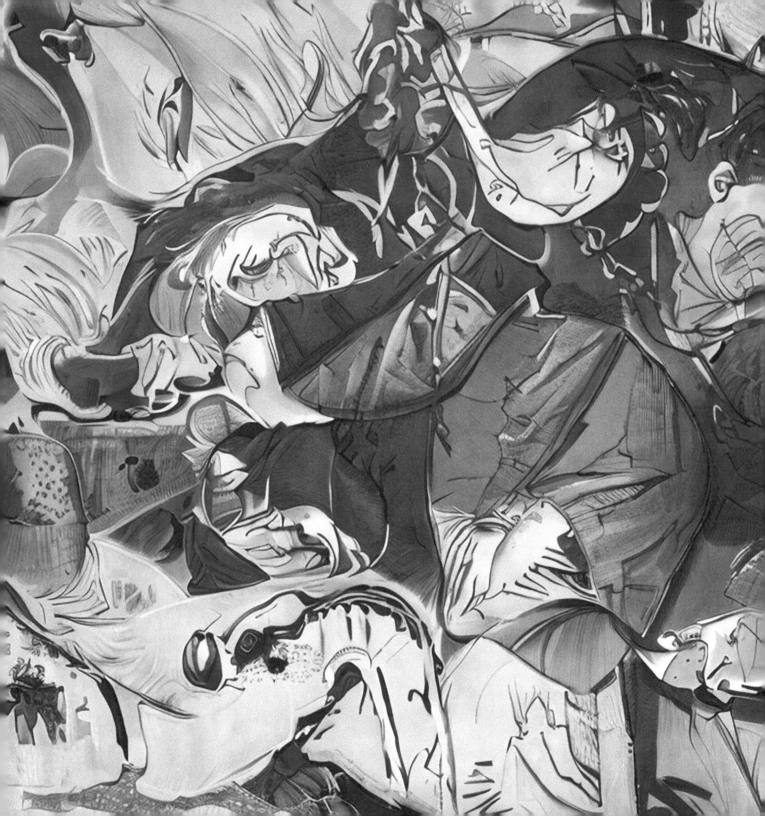

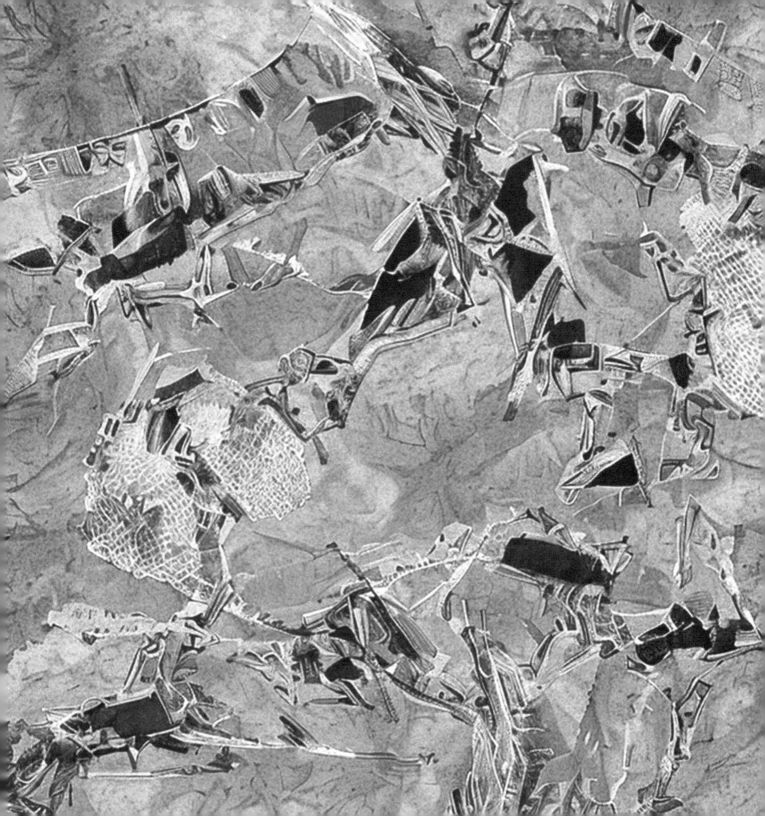

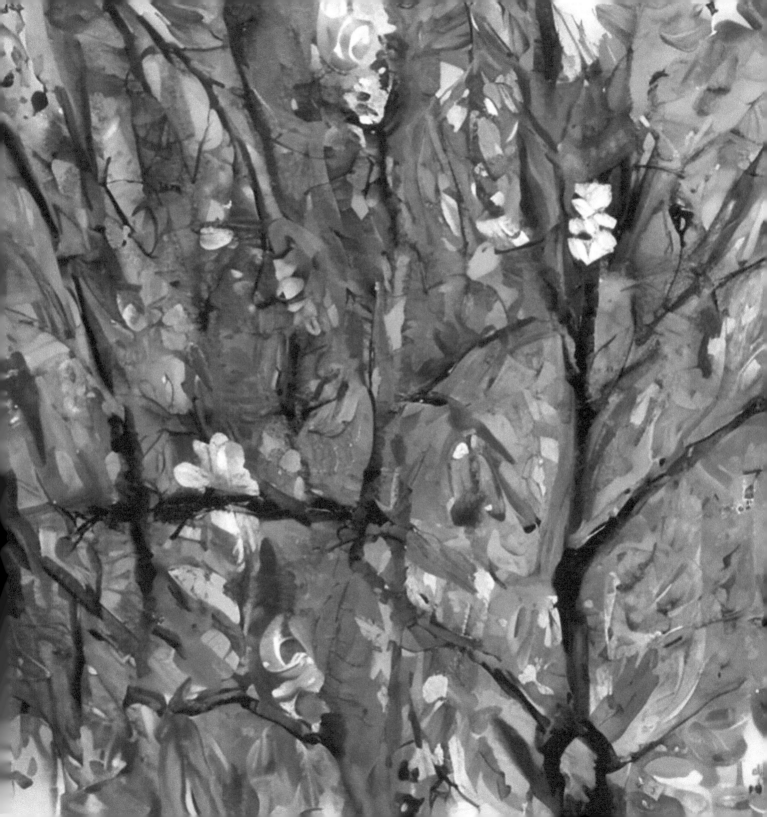

Appendix A:
Eye
Gari

About the Author

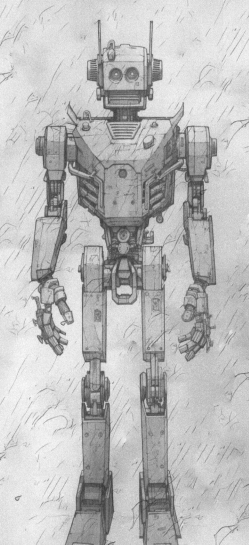

Corey Anton is Professor of Communication Studies at Grand Valley State University and a Fellow of the International Communicology Institute. He is author of *Selfhood and Authenticity* (2001, SUNY Press), *Sources of Significance: Worldly Rejuvenation and Neo-Stoic Heroism* (2010, Purdue University Press), *Communication Uncovered: General Semantics and Media Ecology* (2010, IGS Press), and *How Non-being Haunts Being: On Possibilities, Morality, and Death Acceptance* (2020, Fairleigh Dickinson University Press). He is the editor of *Valuation and Media Ecology: Ethics, Morals, and Laws* (2010, Hampton Press), and the co-editor, along with Lance Strate, of the collection *Korzybski And . . .* (2012, IGS Press), and co-editor, along with Robert K. Logan and Lance Strate, of the collection, *Taking Up McLuhan's Cause* (2017, Intellect Publishing). Past Editor of the journal *Explorations in Media Ecology* and Past President of the Media Ecology Association, Anton currently serves as Vice-President of the Institute of General Semantics, and on the editorial boards of *The Atlantic Journal of Communication, ETC, New Explorations*, and *Explorations in Media Ecology*.

Printed in the USA
CPSIA information can be obtained
at www.ICGtesting.com
JSHW041113111023
49724JS00001B/9